9 STEPS TO

SUCCESSFUL

GOAL ACHIEVEMENT

BY TONY WOODALL

MOTIVATE & INSPIRE OTHERS

SHARE THIS BOOK!

RETAIL PRICE: 7.97 + TAXES AND SHIPPING

SPECIAL QUANTITY DISCOUNTS

10 – 29 BOOKS	$6.97 EACH
30 – 500 BOOKS	$5.97 EACH
501 – 1000 BOOKS	$3.97 EACH

TO PLACE AN ORDER CONTACT:

MOTIVATED ACTION MEDIA, LLC

415-887-0225

info@MotivatedActionMedia.com

DEDICATION

TO MICHAEL BRITO (@Britopian) FOR RE-IGNITING A SPARK

TO JON BERARD AND MAIK PIETSCH FOR YOUR EXHAUSTIVE REVIEW AND EDITS

TO MY MASTERMIND PARTNERS: DAN DURAN AND ANNEMARIE ERBEL FOR KEEPING ME ACCOUNTABLE

TO MY NATIONAL SPEAKERS ASSOCIATION OF NORTHERN CALIFORNIA SPEAKERS ACADEMY MASTERMIND TEAM SUZANNE CAMPI, DR. JACLYN BUETTNER, DC, AND YLMA GUTIERREZ FOR MOTIVATING ME TO GET IT DONE AND KEEPING ME ACCOUNTABLE

THE POWER OF MASTERMIND GROUPS AND ACCOUNTABILITY PARTNERS IS IMMENSE.

TABLE OF CONTENTS

Introduction

Are you one of the millions of people that set New Year's Resolutions?

Did you know that 25% of the people that set New Year's Resolutions quit in the first week?

The majority of the rest of the 75% quit their resolutions within three (3) months.

Do you know what the number one New Year's Resolution is? The winner is – Losing Weight. The fitness center industry loves this time of year. Fitness Center memberships increase as much as 30-50% for some clubs. 50% of all new health club members quit within their first six months.

Regular gym members HATE this time of year.

The lines on the ellipticals and treadmills can be as long as an hour, at some gyms. Lucky for them, 80% of the New Year's Resolution crowd QUITS by the second week of February and by the end of March the gym is back to normal.

This is just for the Weight Loss New Year's "Resolutionist" (NYR). I would imagine the numbers are the same for most NYR's. Why is this?

New Year's Resolutions do not work!

When people start talking about setting New Year's Resolutions at the end of the year and into January, they don't really "SET" anything. They typically just think about them. They talk to their friends and family about what they want to resolve to do over the next year. Other than talking about them, they really don't do much about them.

Why don't they work? They don't work for the majority of people because they don't take the 9 *Steps to Successful Goal Achievement.*

Setting Goals Works!

Goal setting works. It is critical that you set goals, instead of just New Year's Resolutions at the beginning of each year. However, goal setting should be a year-round process.

Wait! You say that you've set goals before and that you never or rarely achieve them? You have set goals and nothing ever happened?

What is the difference between a Goal and a Resolution?

Did you think they are the same? They seem like the same thing. However, in the definitions there is a key difference.

Let's look at the two:

Resolution

a resolve; a decision or determination: "to make a firm resolution to do something."

"His resolution to clear his friend's reputation allowed him to focus on the task."

Goal

the object of a person's ambition or effort, an aim or desired result

"Completing his Certificate in Marketing has become one of the most important goals in his life."

The major emphasis of the two definitions is the word EFFORT in the definition for Goal. A resolution, in itself, is just a decision or maybe a determination.

The concept of a goal is that there is effort involved in the achievement of the goal. That makes sense, right?

"Then why", you ask, "do I still not achieve my goals? I go to the gym and work out, but I still haven't lost the weight that I set as my goal?"

There could be two reasons you don't achieve your goals?

1. You didn't use the 9 Steps to Successful Goal Achievement, or
2. Your subconscious mind is telling you that you can't!

Say What? My subconscious mind is telling me I can't achieve my goals?

Yes! One of the things that can hold you back is the programming in your subconscious mind. Our brains are like computers and are taught many things as we grow up. Even into adulthood we can have things programmed in our subconscious that may be negative to our goals. The mind may think you are already successful; you don't need to achieve that goal.

Goal Setting is a process that, to be successful, you must take certain steps. Some of these steps are basic Goal Achievement processes. Some of these steps must be done to overcome the negative programming in our subconscious mind that inhibits our goal achievement.

Use the 9 Steps to Successful Goal Achievement to turn your New Year's Resolutions into New Year's Realizations!

The Author

When I was young, like most people, I went to school and was taught that I had to go through elementary then secondary school and that I should go on to college to have a good career. I remember studying hard, getting good grades for most of my education. When I was in high school many of my friends were talking about going to college. My best friend, Larry, used to tell me he was going to go to college and become a dentist. I remember him saying that since I met him in the fifth grade.

I didn't have a lot of successful people to hang around with when I grew up. I was raised by a single mom for much of my childhood. My father left before I was born and my first stepfather was an alcoholic. I didn't learn many success-oriented skills as a young child. We moved in with my grandparents along with several of my Mom's sisters and their kids.

My mom later married again and I grew into my teens with a stepfather that was abusive to my Mom, my sister and me. I didn't learn good financial or success-oriented skills during this time, either. I aspired to be successful, however. Knowing that I needed to go to college to get a good job and start a rewarding career, I talked to my parents and grandparents. No one in my immediate family had ever graduated from college.

When I was young, my parents and grandparents told me that I "wasn't college material". They told me I couldn't afford to go to college.

I believed them.

I never felt that I would amount to anything. I would try to do things to better myself. I would set a goal to "be something", but for some reason never achieved it.

I wanted to be successful. I joined the Army National Guard, planning to get the GI Bill to pay my way through college. My grades were good enough to allow me to select the military training I wanted. I selected electronics.

In my electronics course, I wanted to be the top student. I studied hard. I ended up graduating as Distinguished Student – the 2nd highest award. I later learned that National Guard didn't qualify for the GI Bill for education. Well, there goes my college degree, I thought.

I wanted to be successful and earn a lot of money. I started reading motivational books and attending motivation seminars. I went into network marketing and started trying to become successful. While doing all of this, I started studying the motivational speakers and started getting excited about following my dreams.

I had many dreams! None seemed to come true.

I became a Deputy Sheriff after a couple years of not finding a career in electronics repair, something about not having experience. You know the old saying, "How can I get experience if I can't get a job." I wanted to be the top student in the Law Enforcement Academy. I studied hard, worked hard and graduated as the Honor Graduate – the 2nd highest award.

Do you see a pattern forming?

I still wanted to be successful and make more money. I left law enforcement to become a professional speaker presenting crime prevention classes and selling tear gas canisters.

I started learning sales techniques and continued reading motivational books. I attended motivational seminars presented by every motivational speaker I could afford to go to. I traveled out of town and spent the night at cheap motels so I could see and learn from my favorite motivational speakers.

I had a dream! They all said I could achieve my dreams if I only believed. I believed!

I believed, but for some reason, I never achieved.

Do you know someone like this? They listen to motivational speakers, attend motivational seminars, read self-help books, but for some reason never seem to achieve their dreams?

I was that person. Until I figured it out!

In my martial arts training, I learned that the mind can do many things. I learned meditation techniques and other skills to start stretching what my mind thought it could do. But, I wanted to learn more about the mind and how it worked. I enrolled in a hypnosis class at Hypnosis Motivation Institute.

I learned about the brain and how the subconscious mind worked and how it can be programmed starting at an early age with either positive or negative beliefs. I also learned that these beliefs that we think of as negative, may actually be thought of as positive or the truth to the subconscious mind.

I was fascinated by what can be done through hypnosis and wanted to learn more. I completed all of the courses at HMI eventually becoming a Certified Hypnotherapist. I completed a one-year internship working with patients on their goals of weight loss, smoking cessation, etc.

One of the best courses I completed was how to use hypnotherapy-related techniques to overcome the negative programming in our subconscious mind and replace it with positive, success-oriented thoughts and beliefs. Dr. John Kappas, the founder of HMI had been sharing these techniques with his clients, many very successful, for many years.

I started studying goal setting and reading more and more books on successful people. Learning what they did to achieve their success. What they did to achieve their goals. I started taking these lessons and applying them to my own life. I started achieving my goals. I improved my lifestyle, my career, and my income.

As I continued to achieve the goals that I set, I decided I wanted to start sharing these amazing steps and techniques with others. I started developing a course that I started teaching to Realtors, mortgage bankers, and business leaders. I presented the course to Boards of Realtors, civic groups, mortgage lenders, real estate sales people.

I am passionate about coaching people to become the person they want to be, to achieve the goals they set. I took the first part of the Goal Achievement Success System and created this book, 9 Steps to Successful Goal Achievement. I created a podcast, Goal Getting Podcast, to share this information with you. Please go check it out on Apple Podcasts, Spotify, iHeart Radio, Google Play Music and most podcast sites. You can visit my podcast website **www.GoalGettingPodcast.com** to listen to the show.

Podcasting as a goal.

I believe in continuous improvement. I was taking courses in Marketing, a subject that I am very interested in. I was in one of my Social Media Marketing Strategy classes with Michael Brito, who if you saw in the dedication re-ignited a spark I had let dim.

One of my fellow students was sitting behind me and was discussing with another classmate about marketing and radio stations. There was a discussion going on about something in the news related to social media marketing. My friend said,

"I don't listen to radio much anymore. All I listen to are podcasts."

BAM! My brain just started going into a whirlwind. Wait, you used to podcast. I actually started my first podcast in 2004-2005. I thought then this was going to be a big thing. When I left the class I searched on iTunes, where my friend had mentioned he got most of his podcasts, and saw hundreds of podcasts.

After I did more research and learned that podcasting was reaching more people than I could have imagined, I set a new goal.

I will create a podcast where I can share the information I have wanted to share about goal setting and the Goal Getting, Don't Just Set'em Get'em program. The goal was set! The action plan defined and Goal Getting Podcast was conceived.

Let's get started Getting the Goals You Set!

Follow That Dream!

Motivational Speakers were really great about telling you to DREAM BIG!

I love motivational speakers, don't get me wrong. I consider myself to be one as a professional speaker. I have followed many of them over the years. I have many dreams. I have many goals. In this book, you will learn what the difference is between the two.

I have listened to motivational speakers on tapes, CD's, audio books and at many live seminars.

I spent a lot of money and time going to seminars. I got excited, like many people in the audience do.

Have you attended motivational seminars? Have you gotten excited by the things the speaker said?

Some speakers have brought me to tears. I wanted to believe so much in what they were saying! I wanted to achieve my dreams. But, although they excited me, pumped me up, got me motivated, they never really explained HOW TO SET GOALS to achieve these dreams.

One of my favorite motivational speakers and probably the one that had the most impact on my life is Tony Robbins. Several years ago, I attended Tony's Awaken the Fire Within seminar in Atlanta, GA. Tony's seminar and the books and tapes (yes, it was back when there were cassette tapes, not CD or DVD) I purchased taught me many truths about goal achievement and overcoming negative programming. I learned that Tony Robbins is a practitioner of NLP (Neuro-Linguistic Programming) and uses many of these techniques as part of his training programs.

Why is this important?

Many people are "Positive Thinkers" or practice the "Law of Attraction", yet many still fail to achieve their goals.

Why do so few people achieve the goals they set?

- *They Don't Set Their Goals Properly.*
- *They Are Subconsciously Programmed Not to Achieve Them.*

The **9 Steps to Successful Goal Achievement** in this book will teach you proven, systematic techniques and processes to correct these two actions that prevent you from achieving your goals.

In the next chapter we'll talk about *SMART Goals*. As most of you probably know, this is a methodology for understanding the key components that should be included when you are setting goals.

SMART Goals

You may or may not have heard that setting SMART Goals is important. I have heard and recommend the use of the SMART Goals concepts for years. According to every goal setting seminar speaker or book you read they will tell you that your goals should be SMART. SMART stands for:

S = Specific

Goals should be specific, clear and precise. What exactly do you want to accomplish? How can this be accomplished?
"I want to get in shape", is not specific. What is meant by "in shape"?

M = Measurable

Goals must be quantifiable. What has to be done? How do I know when Done Is? What are the specific steps that must be completed so that I can say I accomplished my goal?

A = Achievable

Goals must be able to be accomplished. Winning the Lottery is not a goal! Yes, you could win the lottery, but other than buying the ticket, you cannot do anything to achieve the goal. Lotteries are games of chance. Your goal must be something you can achieve.

R = Realistic

Goals that are realistic are determined by what you are willing and able to do to accomplish them. It is what you really believe you can do. Is it something that with the right amount of belief, work and ability you can achieve?

T = Time-Bound

Goals must have a date attached to them. Goals without a deadline are just dreams! You can and should dream big, but if you don't put a deadline to that dream, it is just that, a dream!

I recently saw where the UC Davis Medical School Employee Development Department had created an extension to the SMART Goals concept. They included two additional concepts to make them SMARTER Goals.

E = Evaluate

Goals should be reviewed regularly and adjusted as necessary. In the LEAN Startup methodology, this is referred to as Pivoting. You should be aware of when changes in life or business require you to change. If you must make a change, do so.

I like this concept because goals should be reviewed not just regularly, but frequently. You don't want them to be "Out of Sight, Out of Mind".

R = Re-Do

Re-Do the SMARTER process after evaluation reveals the need to adjust or pivot. This is a new concept and is sometimes chided by some motivational speakers. You should just push through the obstacles. However, most successful people will tell you that it is better to Fail Often, Fail Fast!

Evaluating and Re-doing are very good concepts. We need to keep our goals top of mind and always be aware of what our next process or activity is. Sometimes it may be necessary to modify your goal or even change it completely.

When I was a Loan Officer back in 2006 – 2009, my goal was to earn the Top Gun award. I wanted to close over $1,000,000 per month. I had started my career as a loan officer in April 2006. By 2008, the real estate market in Georgia had crashed so far that builders were going bankrupt and some of my friends that were closing over $10M per month were now barely doing $1M and they had been working in their field for over 10-20 years.

I had to modify my goals and even pivot my career. I had to take a part-time position in the bakery of a supermarket to pay the bills. I changed my goal to get a position back into the Enterprise Content Management field.

People want to be successful at achieving their goals and these concepts are necessary to do so. Most people know of or have heard of SMART Goals. Yet, most of the people that set goals, even SMART goals, DO NOT ACHIEVE their goals.

WHY NOT? One of the key concepts of SMART goals is that they must be achievable. If they set achievable goals, why don't they achieve them? One of the things we have found is that our subconscious mind is often filled with negative programming that works against us when we try to be successful.

S.M.A.R.T. goals were making me feel D.U.M.B. Are you feeling that way, too? I wasn't dumb and neither are you. What was happening was I "Didn't Understand My Brain. Once I learned what made my brain work and how the subconscious mind worked, I was able to set up the 9 Steps to Successful Goal Achievement and that helped me start to achieve the goals I set. They will work for you as well.

Let's look at the steps you need to take to start turning these negatives into positives.

Step 1 ~ Write It Down!

Napoleon Hill, in his book, <u>Think & Grow Rich</u>, talks about how he interviewed the most successful people of his time. This included people like Andrew Carnegie and J. P. Morgan. As Napoleon Hill interviewed these successful business leaders to learn what made them successful he found one common thread!

Clearly Defined, Written Goals!

In my *Goal Achievement Success System*, the first key step in successful Goal Setting is to write your goals down.

The majority of people do not write their goals down. This is the major problem with New Year's Resolutions. When people set their resolutions at the beginning of the year, they don't really "SET" them. Most people just think about them and say they are going to do them.

Did you know you have a 42% GREATER CHANCE of achieving your goal if you WRITE IT DOWN? Dr. Gail Matthews, a psychology professor at Domincan University in California, performed a study on goal setting. She set up five groups.

Group 1 was asked to just "think about their goals" – what they wanted to accomplish

Groups 2-5 were asked "Write their goals down"

Group 3 was asked to "formulate action commitments"

Group 4 was asked to "formulate action commitments" and "send their goals and action commitments to a supportive friend."

Group 5 was asked to "formulate action commitments" and "send their goals and action commitments AND weekly status reports to a supportive friend."

According to the research, Dr. Matthews found that

The positive effect of <u>Written Goals</u> was supported.

Those who wrote their goals accomplished significantly more than those who did not write their goals.

You can see from the chart above that there is proven truth for the need to write your goals down.

It is also important how you write them down. It is critical to set the goal up in the brain and the subconscious mind. Writing down your goals should be a process that you develop. Napoleon Hill, the author of Think and Grow Rich, emphasises that you should have

Clearly Defined, Written Goals!

What does Clearly Defined mean? It is important to be *specific* when writing down your goals.

Specific is the S in SMART.

"Specific is Terrific"
- Tony Woodall

What are your goals? How would you write them down?

If my goal was to buy a BMW Z4, how would I write that goal down?

"I will purchase a Red BMW Z4 that is less than three years old when I pay off all of my short-term debt."

What does this tell us?

My Z4 will be Red. I will only buy a Z4 that is less than 3 years old, not an old BMW. The most important part here is the terms I must accomplish before I can achieve this goal – when I pay off all of my short-term debt.

Could this be more specific? Could I specify a date when I will pay off my short-term debt? Yes, I could. That may actually be another goal in itself. If you haven't already set a date for paying off that debt, then you need to do that.

Writing down this *Clearly Defined* goal will help me know what I need to DO to achieve this goal.

Clearly Defined, Written Goals are Critical to Getting Your Goals.

Step 2 ~ Be Realistic!

*B*ecoming the Queen of England is probably not a Realistic Goal!

It is important to set up goals that are realistic. **Do Not** set yourself up for failure. Many people set up goals that are not realistic.

Kate Middleton probably never really thought she stood a chance at being the Queen of England. So, it could happen, to her.

Realistic is the R in SMART Goals.

I want to be very careful here. When you set a goal, it shouldn't be easy. When you think of Realistic, many people think that we are saying to be conservative. To just do what you think you can do. That is not true.

You do not want to set goals that are easily achieved. If you do that, then you won't try hard to do it because it isn't out of your comfort zone and that is what you want to do. Set your goal outside of your comfort zone.

The achievement of your goal has to be meaningful. If it doesn't mean something to you, then you won't be motivated to struggle when you get slowed by roadblocks

What do we mean by unrealistic?

Your goals should be based on your knowledge, skills and abilities. If you set a goal that "You want to be a doctor by the end of next year," that may be unrealistic. If you are a senior in high school, well, actually it's delusional, as Michael Hyatt says. We are talking about a big difference. If I said my goal was to win Wimbledon next June, that, if you've watched me play tennis, would also be delusional.

That doesn't mean we shouldn't set "Stretch Goals". We should set goals out of our comfort zone. We should set goals that, if achieved, will mean something.

If you are a sales representative and your goal is to increase your sales by 3%, and you asked yourself, how would you feel about achieving that? If it doesn't make you sweat, then it probably isn't out of your comfort zone. If you set it so high that you cannot in your mind actually believe it, then it is not just out of your comfort zone, it is likely unrealistic.

> **"It is better to aim at the sun and hit an eagle, than aim at an eagle and hit a rock.**
> **- American Indian Proverb**

Make your goals real, but just out of your comfort zone so you have to stretch to achieve them. Make your goal mentally, emotionally or physically significant.

Step 3 ~ Set A Deadline!

Napoleon Hill said it best in 1883.

"A Goal is a Dream with a Deadline.

Without a deadline, it is just a dream!   Without a deadline, there is no pressure! Maybe it gets done, maybe it doesn't.

Time-Based is the T in SMART Goals.

Without a time constraint, it is so easy to say, Yes, I will get around to it. One of the networking groups I was involved in years ago used to give out "Round TUITS" to people that uttered that statement. At that point, they HAD a "Round TUIT and could not say that any longer and were expected to now set a deadline.

What do you set as a deadline? That depends on the goal.

If your goal is something that will take time to achieve, then it is important to break the goal down to Short-Term and Long-Term Goals. If the goal will take many months to even years before you can accomplish it, we will often get discouraged before we achieve the goal without having short-term achievements.

How do you eat an elephant?

The answer is, of course, "One bite at a time!"

You may not be able to sit down and eat it all in one bite, but if you take smaller bites and just keep eating, you will eventually eat the entire elephant.

I recently set a couple of goals that I expect to take 2-3 years to complete. Just having these goals without breaking them down will present a difficulty in seeing the end. When I actually look at the goals, they are easily broken down into several short-term and long-term goals that are still shorter in length than the overall goal.

Breaking them down to smaller bites makes it easier to consume and still want to finish the elephant.

You will find this type of situation when you set career goals or other complex goals that, if you are being realistic, will take some time.

Martial Arts Training

I was actively involved in martial arts for many years. I eventually earned the rank of Godan or 5th Degree Black Belt. I taught classes at our Dojo (martial arts school) in Atlanta and also had several students around the United States that I traveled to and taught. I also performed seminars at the request of other instructors.

When I started, there were 3 belt rankings. You started as a White Belt. After a while (a long while... usually about 1-2 years) you would get promoted to a Green Belt. Finally, after another year or two, you could achieve your Black Belt!

There were not many people that achieved a Black Belt in this program. Many people, many adults, quit before they reached the Black Belt level. After a few years of the art being in America, the Grandmaster of this Japanese martial art changed the structure for advancement.

The ranking levels went from 3 belts / levels to a program that gave short-term goal levels to achieve the long-term Black Belt. The change set everyone starting with the White Belt as usual. The green belt levels were changed to 9 levels. This covered 9 different areas of training for each level. After achieving the 9th green belt level or 1st Kyu ranking, you were ready to move up to the 1st Dan or First-Degree Black Belt rank. This made it much easier to keep students around longer.

Achieving short-term goals helps to maintain motivation for most people. Everyone wants to be a success. Doing small achievements keeps us going forward. Setting deadlines for those short-term goals that lead to long-term achievement is very important.

If your Goal is to be promoted to Black Belt in your martial art, then you should set deadlines to achieve the skills needed to be promoted to the lower level ranks.

For Example –

I will be promoted to my first-degree black belt at next year's December awards ceremony.

I will be promoted one level of the green belt rankings every quarter starting with 1st Kyu at this year's November awards ceremony.

This step is also one of the reasons most New Year's Resolutions fail. The majority of people that set resolutions don't specify a deadline other than "this year".

Step 4 ~ Set an Action Plan!

Setting Goals, like baking, requires you to set up an action plan, or recipe, that should be followed to achieve that goal.

Goals by themselves won't get accomplished by just writing them down. Setting an action plan will include doing all of the things necessary to achieve that goal. You will be analyzing the specific steps that it takes to achieve the goal. A goal requires effort to achieve. It requires action.

"A Goal Without a Plan Is Just a Wish!

- Antoine de Saint-Exupery

Wishing on a star, throwing a penny in a well are all great notions, but life isn't a fairy tale. Dream the dream and work the goal to successful achievement.

My Action Plan to Earn my CMB

One of my goals was to earn the Certified Mortgage Banker designation from the Mortgage Banker Association. My WHY for achieving this goal was to become an industry expert and influencer in the mortgage lending industry.

In 2004, I decided I wanted to earn the CMB and be awarded it at the MBA Convention in October, 2005. I knew it was realistic as I had already achieved many of the requirements I needed. However, it was a stretch goal as I still needed to attend one more course, study for and pass a 6-hour written exam and an oral exam before a board of CMB's. So, I set up an action plan to achieve the rest of the requirements.

The steps I needed to accomplish were:

- Attend School of Mortgage Banking Course III in April
- Study 3 Days per Week
- Obtain the Study Guide after SOMB III
- Talk to Griff, (My Sponsor), at least two times per month
- Find oral and written exam location close by in August.
- Pass Written Exam by September 15th
- Pass Oral Exam by September 30th

These were the specific tasks that I needed to complete my goal within the one-year time frame I had set for my deadline.

When you set goals, you should create an action plan to achieve that goal. If you don't have a plan, you won't know what you must do to achieve that goal.

Set specific steps or actions that you know you need to complete to achieve this goal. I actually knew the steps that were required to achieve my goal before I set the deadline. Since four of my actions were scheduled outside of my control, I had to set my deadline based on those items happening. Setting my deadline sooner than they would be offered would have made the deadline and thus my goal unrealistic.

I completed each of these steps in the allotted timeframes and was awarded my CMB designation at the October 2005 MBA Annual Convention.

Never mistake motion for action

      - Ernest Hemingway

Step 5 ~ Measure It!

"What gets measured gets done!"

- Tom Peters

You must be able to track whether you are achieving success. This is partly because we as humans strive for completion. But, we also get bored easily. We must be able to track how we are doing. Little steps mean a lot.

Measurable is the M in SMART Goals.

Our social structure is based on us measuring our actions. In school we are "Graded" F – A, worst to first. We even go further with plus and minus grades... *Is A Plus really that much better than A Minus. Isn't an A good enough?*

We often get asked, "On a scale of 1 – 10, how would you rate this?" These days we rate by Likes or Favorites. People on Facebook or Twitter count the number of Likes or Favorites they get to rank how they are doing. In social media, you are ranked by Twitter followers, Klout & Kred scores, etc.

After you set up your action plan you will want to track and measure those tasks that lead to the short-term and long-term goals. How do you measure them? Do you put a Score on each one?

In 2006, when my dream job was eliminated, the company I worked for allowed me to start my new career as a Loan Officer, another goal of mine. They paid for me to attend Xinnix – The Mortgage Academy to get the training I needed to become a great loan officer.

At Xinnix, we learned to set specific goals for specific actions that we had to perform that were required to succeed as a Loan Officer.

Xinnix used an aviation or "Top Gun" type of motivational concept for students. Many mortgage companies, as well as other sales-based companies, use this type of theme.

Those sales persons that meet or exceed their goals are awarded the Top Gun Award. The company I worked for used this motivational tool for their loan officers. Those that earned their Top Gun Award also got additional benefits such as a being a member of the Champions Club and a spot on the Champions Club trip.

This became my goal as a loan officer:

I will become a Top Gun at my company at the end of this year and attend the Champions Club trip in March.

Using this type of TOP GUN concept, actions are broken into three groups – PRE-FLIGHT, IN-FLIGHT and POST

FLIGHT. Each group had specific actions that should be accomplished for success in pre-sales, during sales and post-sales process.

It is important that you set a goal for each action. Remember we are defining measurable actions that have to be achieved for success.

One of our action steps was to make a 40 Database Calls (calls to prospects on your list – your target market) per week. That breaks down to 8 per day, Monday – Friday.

We assigned an amount of MILEAGE, to each action. Pilots love to get mileage. They track their experience and success by the number of miles flown in the pilot seat. In our tracking, each action is given mileage points that are based on the importance of the task.

Let's look at some other examples that might be used:

Pre-Flight Task	Goal	Mileage
Database Calls	40 / Week	3
Key Target Visits	15 / Week	10
Builder / Attorney Visits	1 / Week	15
Agent Training / Seminar	1 / Week	25

You can see on this example that the mileage for making calls and presenting an Agent Training or Seminar are a lot different; 25 miles vs. 3 miles each. This is because of the benefit gained by each.

Therefore, when you are assigning points, miles, or dollars for each action completed, think about the importance or benefit for each action.

If I perform this action, how will it affect the overall achievement of my ultimate goal? If the completion of an action is more important or difficult to accomplish, reward yourself with a higher measurement.

At the end of each day, we should count the totals. Our weekly goal was a 500-point minimum. Yes, you could and I often tried to exceed that minimum. We rated ourselves each day with an A for meeting 100+ miles daily or B for 50 – 100 miles.

At the end of the week, we want to total each category. We tracked the total miles to date as well as average weekly mileage.

This concept was carried over after Xinnix Training by me and most other graduates. When I started my loan origination business I continued to use this methodology.

I actually prefer to use currency for tracking and measuring. Most people understand the concept of money and believe that the more money they have, the more successful they are. That might not be true, but it is the perception of most people and society in general.

Instead of mileage, assign dollar values to the tasks completed. Total the dollars at the end of each day and the end of the week.

Let's take a look at a simple chart that you can use to measure your progress through the days of the week.

Date Range 1/05/2018 - 1/11/2018	Goal	Reward	MON	TUE	WED	THU	FRI	SAT	SUN	Totals	Target Goal
Major Steps											
Calorie Intake	1200/Day	200	200	200	200	200	200	200	200	1400	1,400
Calories Burned	2200/Day	200	200	200	200	200	200	200	200	1400	1,400
Calorie Deficit	1000/Day	300	300	300	300	300	300	300	300	2100	2,100
Action Steps											
Cardio										0	
Elliptical (1 Hour each level 5)	3 / wk	100	100		100		100			300	300
Walk / Run (Sat/Sun - 5 Miles)	2/days / wk	200						200	200	400	400

In the chart, I have used dollar amounts to measure my progress. Assign a dollar value to each action step. In my goal to lose weight, I have set up my major steps: The key elements that need to be met for weight loss (Calorie Intake, Calories Burned and Calorie Deficit). If I achieve each one of those I pay myself a certain amount. For instance, if I achieve my calorie intake of 1200 and that's not a minimum, but a maximum, I will earn $200. If I burn 2200 calories per day, I earn $200. I also earn money for each action step that I take to achieve those major steps. You get the picture, right?

If you want to learn more about this method of incentive of building a mental bank account, contact me to sign up for coaching in the Goal Achievement Success System.

"What gets measured gets done. What gets measured and fed back gets done well. What gets rewarded gets repeated.

- John E. Jones

Are You Getting the Goals You Set?

We have covered the first 5 of the key steps to setting goals in the **9 Steps to Successful Goal Achievement, taught in my Goal Achievement Success System.**

Do you know anyone that has set their goals and never achieved them?

Have you tried to achieve goals and it seems that you quickly lose focus or start thinking, *"I am never going to achieve this goal."*

Do you read motivational books or listen to motivational speakers on podcasts, or audiobooks on your smartphone or tablet? Do you get excited and then later after start thinking, *"I'll never achieve that, I've never achieved any goal I set!"*

Has your subconscious mind been programmed with negative beliefs that may be holding you back?

Do you want to learn how you can reset your mind with the positive success achieving thoughts and beliefs that will allow you to Get the Goals You Set?

The Goal Achievement Success System is designed with two key elements to counter those two "Goal Killers".

It is a program designed to teach you the correct method required to set goals along with a program to tap into your subconscious mind, modify negative programming with positive success-oriented programming that will set you on a path to success.

- You will start to achieve your goals and dreams.
- You will replace those negative limiting beliefs.
- You will kick the Impostor out of your brain.
- You will be successful in being who you want to be.

You will learn proven, systematic techniques designed to help you to **Get the Goals You Set!**

The methods taught in the **Goal Achievement Success System** are proven techniques developed over 30 years. We have presented this program to Realtor's as a continuing education program, to Chambers of Commerce, Mortgage Companies, etc.

One of my coaching clients Ouida, sent me a text with good news the other day. We worked on her goals using the 9 Steps to Successful Goal Achievement and the Goal Achievement Success System program.

It is exciting when someone you work with sends you a text one day saying she has some exciting news to share and the next day you get the great news. Goal Getting works!

You will find in the 9 Steps that you should have an accountability partner. As your coach I work closely to help you define your goals, set your action plan and then I keep you accountable for the work you must do. Once you understand how to use the 9 Steps to Successful Goal Achievement you can then overcome the limiting beliefs, you can work the plan and you, too, can text me the exciting news that YOU are Getting the Goals You Set!

My client and friend, Ouida, is an amazing Wellness Coach. We worked on her goal to build her brand and open her own boutique fitness gym.

> **Hey! It's Ouida. My exciting news is, I'm currently negotiating a lease to open a boutique Fitness gym in Roswell. I'm both excited and scared. It's my ultimate goal to get** 😊

> **Thank you for all of your advice and goal getting strategies! They work!**

Contact me by email at **Tony@GoalGettingPodcast.com** to set up a free Coaching Consultation Call. Be prepared to start achieving your goals.

Visit us at **www.GoalGettingPodcast.com**, our Goal Getting Podcast website to be motivated, learn from experts how they achieved their goals as they share their tips, strategies and inspirational stories.

"The first step to getting somewhere is to decide you aren't going to stay where you are."

- J. P. Morgan

Step 6 ~ Define Your Why!

What is your motivation for setting your goal or goals? What is your WHY? WHY are you trying to achieve the goal(s)? Before you can achieve your goals, and even before you set your goals, you should know exactly why you want to achieve these goals.

Knowing your WHY will help you stay motivated when you are having a bad day and want to quit. Know the true purpose of your path.

This is, by far, the most important concept in Goal Setting I ever came upon.

I worked hard on many goals in my life. I measured and tracked them. I had clearly defined, written goals with specific action plans. Still, it was tough sometimes when things got rough. I would struggle to maintain my focus, I would come up with excuses to procrastinate or not perform the actions I needed to in order achieve my goals. I would lose my way. I heard this quote the other day from Michael Hyatt and it resonates so well.

**"People lose their way
when they lose their why!"**
- Gloria Hyatt

By defining your WHY, you will know what is motivating you. You will then understand what you need to think about when you start hitting the obstacles to achieving your goals.

What is motivating you to attempt this goal? Why do you want to do it? You may need to ask yourself Why? Why? Why? before you get to the real reason. It's kind of like doing a root cause analysis in project management.

In Lean Six Sigma methodology, they use an Ishikawa or "Fishbone" diagram to get to the root cause of a problem. We are taught that it takes about 5 Why's to get to the root cause of almost every problem. It might sound like you are talking to a three-year-old, but it is important to get the true reason for the problem.

In the case of goals and knowing your Why, it may take that many as well. If your goal is to lose weight, ask yourself:

"Why do I want to lose Weight?"

You might answer, "I want to weigh less."

"Why do you want to weigh less?"

"Because if I weigh less, I will feel better."

"Why do you want to feel better?"

"Because, if I feel better, I will be able to do more activities."

"Why do you want to be able to do more activities?"

"Because if I can do more activities, I will be able to spend more time with my family."

So maybe your WHY for losing weight is to be able to spend more time with your family. That WHY is more likely to motivate you than just "wanting to lose weight." When you get down or discouraged while trying to achieve your weight loss goal, you might continue and resist eating bad foods if you are able to start thinking about how you will be able to spend more time with your family when you achieve the weight loss goal.

Knowing your WHY for doing something will motivate you more than just knowing WHAT you want to accomplish.

Define Your Why!

Knowing your WHY will propel you through the tough times and motivate you to achieve your goals. Write your WHY below for your most important goal you are working on. Why do you want to achieve this goal?

"You miss 100% of the shots you don't take."

- Wayne Gretsky

Step 7 ~ Visualize It!

With a clearly defined, written goal we know what our goal is and what we need to do to achieve it. Visualizing your goal and your WHY will work together to put that positive thought of achieving that goal into your subconscious mind.

Our mind is very visual. If you follow social media, you will hear and see that all platforms are getting more visual. The reason for that is we want to see more, not just read more. Our brain is very visually oriented.

In social media, people skim. Bloggers are recommended to put images on their blog and to make shorter paragraphs to make it easier for people to skim the information on their blog.

There are several visualization techniques to get a visual image in your mind. For some people, it may be difficult to imagine things in their mind. This isn't a problem; it may just be the way their brain works. There are techniques you can use to compensate for this.

What you can do is set up visual pictures or cues to help you think about and see yourself with the accomplishment of the goal.

One of my favorite techniques is to put yourself in it.

If your goal is to own a BMW Z-4, go for a test drive in one at your local BMW dealership. Have someone, the salesperson for instance; take a picture of you in the driver's seat of the car. It would be great if you can have it taken while on the road driving it.

When I set this as one of my goals, I went to the BMW Performance Center in Spartanburg, SC and was able to drive around the track in a Z4. My friend, Greg, went with me and took this picture of me in it.

If you cannot put yourself "in the goal", you could set up a GOAL or VISION BOARD / BOOK. Put clippings, photos, positive thoughts or quotes together on a board you can hang up somewhere and see every day.

It will help you to maintain your motivation if you can get a glance of your goal or your Why. Photos of the goals you are trying to achieve will work wonders to keep your eye on the prize.

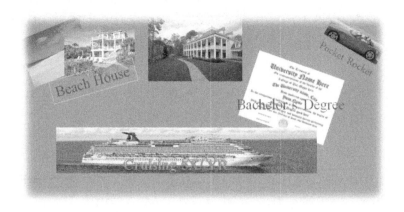

The closer you can put yourself into the photos, the better. You can set up a Vision Board and hang on your wall, you could put it into a Book, or create a Pinterest Board and Pin all of the photos that motivate you or you could do all of the above. Check into your Pinterest board daily to view your visions. The key is to create a visual reminder of what is important to you. Our brains are very visual; use that as a tool to maintain your motivation.

What are some goals you want to achieve? Can you find a picture of it? Can you take a picture of yourself in it, with it, on it? Build that vision board and be visual.

Chase down your passion like it's the last bus of the night.

- Terri Guillemets

Step 8 ~ Make a Commitment!

When you think of contracts what do you think of?

Why do we enter into contracts? When we sign a contract, we enter into a commitment to fulfil a promise to do something.

When I enter into a contract, I make a commitment to fulfil that contract. I make a promise to do what I have agreed to do.

I give you my word that I will perform the actions necessary to complete this contract.

I attended a seminar where the owner of a very successful collection firm was speaking. In explaining how his firm is so successful he said the FIRST step they use when calling someone that is late with a payment is:

"Mr. Smith, I am calling to find out when you are planning to make the payment on the item . . . LIKE YOU PROMISED?

Most of us, since childhood, hold a promise close to heart. How many times did you "Pinky Swear" or "Cross My Heart" when you promised your best friend you would do something.

In the past, and for many in today's society, **"My Word Is My Bond!"** still holds true. You used to never have to sue to collect what was owed you from others. You never had to even write a contract. Your word was your bond. Your PROMISE was good enough.__That is why when we started writing contracts to repay someone, they were written as a "Promissory Note". Many mortgage notes today are still called Promissory Notes.

A contract is a promise. You believe in keeping your promise, don't you?

Make a contract with yourself. Hold yourself accountable. If you wrote a contract with yourself, you will have a stronger chance of keeping that promise. Our mind works better to stick to things we have a contract to repay. What should you do? Write a contract with yourself.

Below we provide an example of a Personal Contract you can create with yourself to make that commitment you need to be successful at achieving your goals.

Hold yourself accountable. Involve others in your commitment. Find a Mentor, A coach, a Mastermind Group or a close friend* to hold you accountable.

If you remember back in Step 1 ~ Write It Down, we were talking about the research project performed by Dr. Gail Matthews at Dominican University in California. In this study, Dr. Matthews and her team proved that writing your goals down gave you a 42% greater chance in achieving your goals.

What their study also showed was that:

- The positive effect of accountability was supported: the people who sent weekly progress reports to their friend accomplished significantly more than those who did not write their goals down, or those who wrote their goals, and did not send make a commitment or send reports to a friend.

- **There was support for the role of public commitment:** those who sent their commitments to a friend accomplished significantly more than those who did not.

This study provides empirical evidence for the effectiveness of three coaching tools: accountability, commitment and writing down one's goals.

Check out the study online to learn how much more effective your goal setting will be when you use accountability, action steps and writing your goals down.

Hanging around like-minded people will help you to maintain the motivation you need to achieve your goals. You will gain positive, well-meaning advice as well.

Jim Rohn is often quoted, "You are the average of the five people you spend time with." It is important to find like-minded people and form a Mastermind. This is one of the keys that Napoleon Hill learned and shared in "Think & Grow Rich."

It is much easier to take the prodding of someone you respect when you get unmotivated or feel you need to get away from your commitment.

*Be careful who you tell your goals to and who you choose to hold you accountable. Sometimes your best friend or even family can be negative when they don't realize it or when they don't mean to.

Some people can be real energy drainers. I call these people **"Ampires"**, because they suck the energy from you like a vampire sucks blood. It is really important that you find someone that is like minded.

If you think about something day and night, every waking moment, and it makes you happy.

You should be doing that.

- Unknown

Step 9 ~ Reward Yourself!

CONGRATULATIONS
YOU ARE A SUCCESS

Rewarding Yourself? What does that have to do with "setting" goals?

It doesn't have anything to do with goal setting. But it does have a lot to do with Goal Getting!

Many of the goals that you are setting are goals that require a change of a habit or habits. Understanding habits and how they are formed, what causes you to adopt that habit and how you respond to the habits will give you an understanding of why rewards are important.

If your goal is to stop smoking or to lose weight, these are typically habits. To change the habit, you must understand the habit and why you do what you do.

According to *The Power of Habit – Why We Do What We Do in Life and Business* by Charles Duhigg, "habits are a three-step loop – Cue – Routine – Reward. This loop, over time, becomes more and more automatic. Eventually the Cue and Reward become intertwined until a powerful sense of anticipation and craving emerges."

This is a great book to read and understand how to change these habits. We use Rewards as a way to help build new habits when we achieve success. Build new Cues, New Routines and New Rewards. Build new success habits.

It is important to maintain our motivation throughout the goal achievement process. If you don't keep yourself motivated and interested in the plan, then you may get frustrated and quit. This is one of the main reasons for Defining Your Why.

We don't want to give up, so we want to use our motivation to keep us on the road to success.

Rewards are important in human culture. Well, actually in all cultures. Dogs are trained more effectively with positive training techniques. Dogs love to get rewarded when they do something good.

Some of the most popular shows on television are the awards shows:

- The Oscars
- The VMA – Video Music Awards
- The Tonys
- The Emmys
- The Grammys

We really like to watch others win awards. We like it because it is a way for us to dream about winning our own awards. We all want to win the MVP in sports, to win a Grammy for Best New Artist, you name it and it is something we all dream about.

So, why not reward yourself with an award when you accomplish those smaller goals. If one of your goals, like mine, is to own a Red BMW Z4 when I pay off all of my credit card bills, then we need to pay ourselves when we achieve things like paying off a credit card or getting the balance down to a specific amount.

When you succeed, go to a local BMW Dealership and take a Test Drive in a new Z4. Or if you have one, visit a BMW Performance Center like I did. The Spartanburg, SC Center has a great track to race Z4's around as well as many different great BMW's.

CONGRATULATE YOURSELF

Reward Yourself for Successes. Even Small Successes!

Write down a few rewards for the goals you are currently working on.

1.

2.

3.

4.

5.

6.

7.

8.

9.

10.

Ready for Success?

Setting goals is not only recommended, it is critical for successful achievement of your goals. As we have mentioned several times in this book, sometimes negative thoughts and beliefs may have found a way into our subconscious mind.

These negative thoughts and beliefs may be part of your life and you may not even know it. This may have been done by your parents, friends, relatives or just from situations we were involved in as we grew up. I learned about these issues we face while learning hypnotherapy. It was amazing to learn what may have held me back from being the success I had intended to be.

While I continued to learn the techniques to correct these negative thoughts and beliefs in my own mind, I also started to test them on myself. Using the techniques that I later used to create **The Goal Achievement Success System**, I was able to successfully achieve the goals I set for myself that ended up **increasing my income 400%**.

Do you have goals that you want to achieve but have had problems doing so? Do you feel like you are failing when it comes to Goal Setting?

Using the techniques in the Goal Getting, Don't Just Set'em, Get'em Program, you can set up your subconscious mind to respond to positive, goal-oriented, successful thoughts and beliefs.

You can achieve the goals you set. We want to help you to reverse that negative and success stealing programming in your subconscious mind. We developed The **Goal Achievement Success System** so that it could be done by anyone.

Setting your goals correctly is just the first step, but a very important one. If you think you will have trouble setting your goals correctly, we offer One-on-One Coaching to walk you through it. We want to help you succeed at **Setting Goals** and we want to see you **Successfully Achieve Your Goals.**

To learn more about the Goal Achievement Success System:

Visit us on our podcast website at **www.GoalGettingPodcast.com**

You can reach me on the Goal Getting Podcast website or at these locations:

To book Tony for Speaking Engagements, call me at 1+ (415) 857-0225 or email at Tony@TonyWoodall.com

Check out my speaker page:

Follow us on Social Media

9 TO SUCCESSFUL GOAL ACHIEVEMENT

STEPS

1. WRITE IT DOWN
2. BE REALISTIC
3. SET A DEADLINE
4. SET AN ACTION PLAN
5. MEASURE IT / TRACK IT
6. DEFINE YOUR WHY
7. VISUALIZE IT
8. MAKE A COMMITMENT
9. REWARD YOURSELF

Made in the USA
Las Vegas, NV
10 December 2021

36846291R00039